Beautiful Beads and Embellishments

Irène Lassus and Marie-Anne Voituriez

David & Charles

ACKNOWLEDGEMENTS

TOUT À LOISIRS
50, rue des Archives
75004 Paris
Tel.: 01 48 87 08 87

LOISIRS ET CRÉATIONS
53, rue de Passy
75016 Paris
Tel.: 01 42 15 13 43
A list of addresses for Loisirs et Créations' 12 sales outlets
can be obtained by calling 01 41 80 64 00

Chief Editor: Catherine Franck
Editor: Valérie Gendreau
Modelling: Agnès Frégé
Diagrams: Patricia Ferreira-Gonçalves
Photography: Cactus Studio, Fabrice Besse
Stylist: Sonia Roy
Revision and Correction: Julien Ringuet
Technical Co-ordinator: Anne Raynaud
Photoengraving: Nord Compo

A DAVID & CHARLES BOOK

First published in the UK in 2004
Originally published as *Perles et paillettes brodées* by Dessain et Tolra, France 2002

Copyright © Dessain et Tolra / VUEF 2002, 2004

Distributed in North America
by F&W Publications, Inc.
4700 East Galbraith Road
Cincinnati, OH 45236
1-800-289-0963

A catalogue record for this book is available from the British Library.

ISBN 0 7153 1796 2

Printed in China by SNP Leefung
for David & Charles
Brunel House   Newton Abbot   Devon

Visit our website at www.davidandcharles.co.uk

David & Charles books are available from all good bookshops; alternatively you can contact our Orderline on (0)1626 334555 or write to us at FREEPOST EX2110, David & Charles Direct, Newton Abbot, TQ12 4ZZ (no stamp required UK mainland).

Contents

Key to symbols

Easy

Of moderate difficulty

Complicated

Inexpensive

Reasonable

Fairly expensive

DECORATIVE FEATURES

ACCESSORIES

CLOTHING

A guide to the cost of each project is given beside the list of materials on the pages indicated above. These figures take into account the cost of support materials (canvas, T-shirts, trousers).

Introduction

Embroidering with beads is an ancient craft combining fabrics, threads and beads.

Today, designs using beads and other embellishments such as sequins and jewels are increasingly popular. Each piece of embellished fabric demonstrates a particular technique: individually embroidered beads or beads that form part of a design; embroidery stitches on canvas; rows of sequins or shisha embroidery which uses tiny mirrors set within embroidered circles. Sometimes even the thread itself takes on a decorative function.

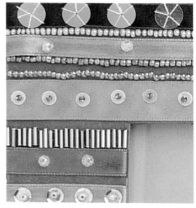

The sources of inspiration are global:

they include African, Indian and North American embroidery, traditional designs from Central Europe and the Middle East and pieces by contemporary Western designers.

Beads come in a host of different materials
and colours for you to create your own long- or short-
term projects, be they straightforward or intricate.

Basic equipment

1 NEEDLES: the size of your needle should be dictated by the thickness of your thread. For beadwork, use a long, fine needle.

2 THREADS AND EMBROIDERY THREADS/SILKS: the latter are made up of six strands which can be easily separated according to the thickness of the embroidery work to be done. They come in a wide range of colours and have an incredible sheen.

3 EMBROIDERY SCISSORS: used for precise cutting and trimming work.

4 TAPE MEASURE: for taking neck, wrist, waist and other measurements.

5 EMBROIDERY HOOP: an essential tool for embroidering on canvas. Place the canvas on the smaller circle, push the larger circle into position and tighten with the screw to hold the fabric secure.

6 CANVAS: for creating extensive stretches of embroidery. Ensure that you always choose a gauge suited to the size of your beads.

7 IRON-ON FABRIC: comes in a variety of colours. Ironed on to the reverse of fabric, it stiffens and prevents fraying.

8 WADDING: used for padding fabrics and for achieving quilted effects.

9 FLEXIBLE MIRROR: can be easily cut and used to create shisha mirrors (see page 14).

10 WASHERS: small drilled out discs available from hardware stores. Used for creating small mirrors (see page 14).

11 BUTTONS: when used unconventionally, pearlised, antique, clear and coloured buttons can assume a decorative role.

12 FABRIC GLUE: for assembling different elements.

13 DRESSMAKER'S PENCILS AND PENS: for outlining designs.

Fabric and ribbons

LACE: sold by the metre (foot) and available in cotton and synthetic materials.

COTTON VOILES: these lightweight coloured fabrics make for interesting games with transparency and colour.

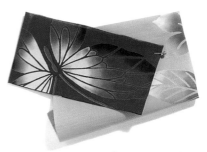

PRINTED FABRICS: these come in a limitless variety of designs, over which you can embroider with beads and sequins.

RIBBONS AND STITCHED SEQUINS: ribbons come in velvet, satin, grosgrain, sheer and other types. Sequins sold by the metre (foot) come pre-stitched together.

FLEECE: shares the same advantages as felt, primarily that it does not fray, but is warmer and more supple.

COTTON FABRICS: readily available and easy to mix and match, cottons come in a wide variety of colours.

ORGANZA AND ORGANDIE: organza is a type of thin silk netting and organdie a type of thin cotton netting. They are lightly stiffened.

FELT: comes in a wide variety of colours. Its greatest attribute is that it does not fray.

SILK: the shiny and precious look of silk makes it ideal for use in bead and sequin work.

Beads and sequins

SMALL CLEAR GLASS BEADS: small glass beads in a variety of colours; the smallest glass beads are used in embroidery work.

FACETED BEADS: in plastic or glass, these are made in many different colours and sizes. They also come in iridescent finishes.

FACETED SEQUINS WITH CENTRE HOLES: may be clear, opaque, shiny or iridescent, and come in a wide variety of sizes and colours.

SMALL OPAQUE GLASS BEADS: come in gold and silver, too. These are used to accentuate the outlines of designs.

BUGLES (LONG BEADS): in embroidery these are used either as flower stems or laid out side by side. They can be used alongside other beads in designs involving fringes.

SEQUINS WITH SIDE HOLES: ideal for making hanging pendants and in fringe work.

STUDS AND SEW-ON JEWELS: come in a variety of shapes, sizes and colours.

FLAT SEQUINS: these are especially suitable for creating scales and flat decorative effects.

ROUND BEADS: can be alternated with small glass beads to create interesting decorative effects.

Chain stitch and lazy daisy stitch

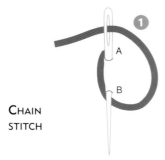

CHAIN STITCH

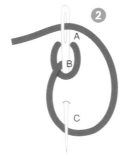

LAZY DAISY STITCH

1 Bring the needle up at A, then insert back into A and bring out at B. Carry the thread under the point of the needle.

2 Pull the thread through and insert the needle back into B. Bring out at C, carrying the thread under the point of the needle.

3 Sew a detached chain stitch by repeating step 1. Pull the thread tight and sew a small stitch to hold the loop in place. Stitch five loops in a circle to create a flower.

Blanket stitch

TECHNICAL TIP
The main difficulty with this stitch is keeping the stitch height even. It may help to faintly draw out two guide lines on the material.

Work from left to right, ensuring that the stitches are kept taut – but not so taut that the fabric crumples. The stitches should be

evenly spaced; ensure that you keep the same distance between each one.

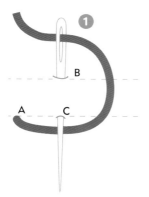

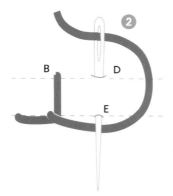

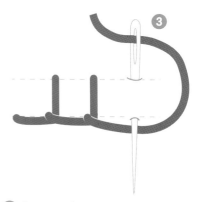

1 Bring the needle up at A, then in again at B. Come up at C, in line with A. Pull through, carrying the thread under the point of the needle.

2 Insert the needle at D, in line with B. Come up at E, carrying the thread under the point of the needle.

3 Repeat this pattern as you work along the row, keeping the stitches even and carrying the thread under the point of the needle.

Herringbone stitch

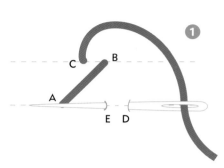 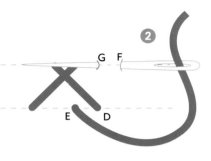 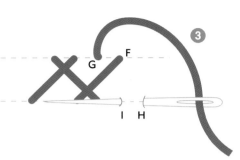

1 Bring the needle up at A, insert at B and come up at C. Insert needle at D and come out at E. The threads should cross close to the upper line.

2 Take a slanting stitch and insert needle at F, come out at G. Pull the needle through. The threads should cross close to the lower line.

3 Come back and insert needle at H, come out at I. Continue in this way, repeating steps 1 and 2.

Fly stitch

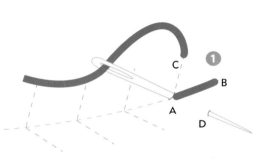 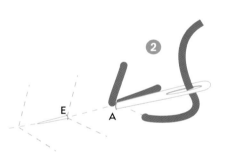

1 Bring the needle up at A on the central line of the motif. Insert needle at B, come out at C and insert again at A. This time, come up at D.

2 Insert back into A and come up at E on the central line, ready for the next set of stitches. Repeat step 1, starting from point B.

WASHING RECOMMENDATIONS
Embroidered clothes and accessories may be washed by hand or by machine. Ensure that you wash them inside out to protect the beads and sequins, or better still, place them in a special bag before putting them in the machine.

Ladder stitch

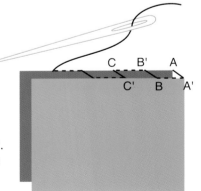

This is used principally for stitching together two pieces of fabric using a stitch concealed in folded fabric, such as a hem.

Insert the needle at A, then into A'. Come out at B, passing the needle under the fold in the fabric. Take the needle in again at B'. Repeat pattern until the row is completed.

Magical window ★★★

MATERIALS REQUIRED

TROPICAL SCENE WINDOW

- *15cm (6in) square of 14-gauge canvas*
- *dressmaker's pencil*
- *3 × 25.5cm (1¼ × 10in) flexible mirror*
- *small glass beads in midnight blue, pale blue, blue, dark blue, gold, silver and bronze*
- *8.5cm (3¼in) square window (inner dimensions)*
- *fabric glue*
- *box frame surround*
- *acrylic paint in ultramarine*
- *paintbrush*
- *fine needle and white thread*

PALM TREE

- *0.3mm (¹⁄₆₄in) enamelled wire*
- *pliers and jewellery glue*
- *small glass beads in bronze and pale green*
- *3 faceted beads in purple*
- *faceted sequins in green*

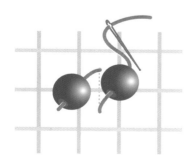

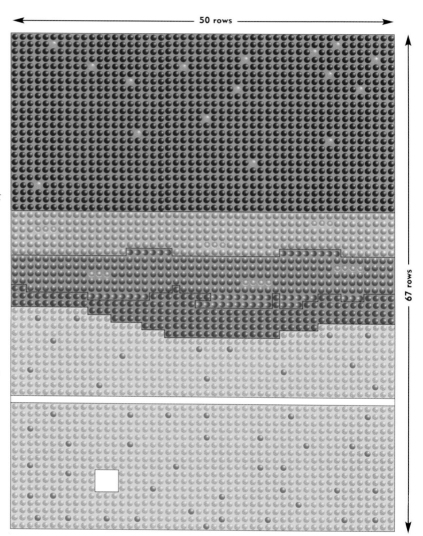

50 rows

67 rows

1 Use a dressmaker's pencil to draw a rectangle 67 rows by 50 in the centre of your canvas. Mark in the blank line and square.

The blank line is where the canvas folds and the square holds the base of the palm tree.

2 Following the pattern shown above, and starting at the top of the rectangle, embroider the beads on to the canvas (see diagram left).

3 Cut and stick strips of flexible mirror to the sides and top of the inside of the window. Cut the canvas 1cm (³⁄₈in) from the beads. Fold under and stick down the excess material on the back of the canvas.

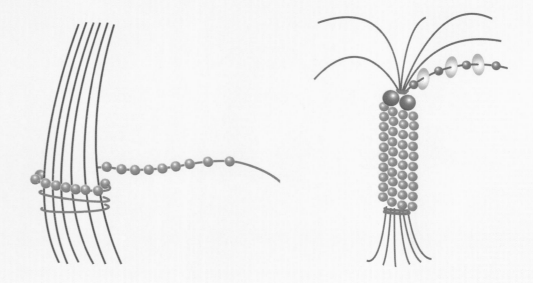

④ To make the palm tree: cut 6 x 15cm (6in) lengths of enamelled wire plus an extra 50cm (20in) length. Bunch the six wires together and secure them with two loops of the long wire 5cm (2in) from their base.

⑤ Thread bronze beads on to the long wire and, keeping it taut, wind the wire gradually around the six wires to form a trunk 3.5cm (1½in) long. Next, thread on the three large purple beads for coconuts and finish with two tight loops around the bunched wires. Trim the end of the long wire.

⑥ To make the palm tree branches, thread alternate green sequins and beads on to each length of enamelled wire over approximately 2.5cm (1in). Finish off by gluing the final bead to the sequin beside it. Wait until the glue is thoroughly dry then trim off the excess wire.

🌙 For a shiny and smooth surface, ensure that you choose a gauge of canvas that is suitable for beadwork – 14-gauge or 18-gauge are good for bead embroidery.

⑦ Trim the wires to an equal length 2.5cm (1in) from the base of the trunk and thread them through the blank square in the canvas; bend the ends of the wires on to the back of the canvas.

⑧ Apply glue to the back and base of the inside of the window and stick the canvas and palm tree on to it. Paint the box frame surround in ultramarine, leave to dry then place the exotic window design inside the box frame.

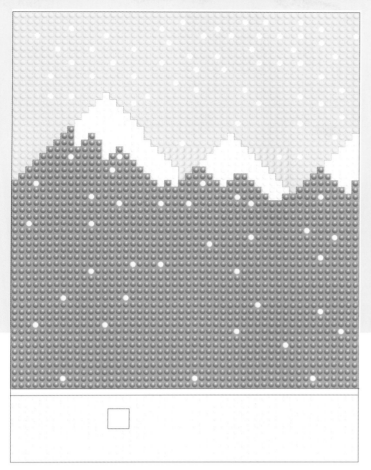

MATERIALS REQUIRED

CHRISTMAS SCENE WINDOW
- *small glass beads in pale blue, pearlized white, blue, dark green and bronze*

CHRISTMAS TREE
- *glass beads in dark green and bronze*
- *faceted sequins in green*
- *small round beads in green*

❶ Embroider the scene following the pattern above and trim the canvas (see page 10, steps 1–3).

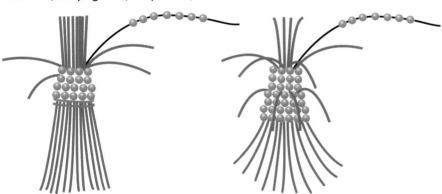

❷ To make the Christmas tree: cut 12 x 15cm (6in) lengths of enamelled wire plus a 50cm (20in) length. Bunch the twelve wires together and secure with two loops of the long wire. Thread on bronze beads over four loops, keeping the wire tight. Next, separate out four of the twelve wires: these will be the lower branches of the tree.

❸ Continue threading bronze beads on to the long wire and wrap it three times around the eight remaining wires. Secure with a loop of long wire and separate out another four strands from the bunched wires. Thread on another four loops of bronze beads and secure with two tight loops of long wire, then pull out the remaining four strands to make the top branches.

❹ Thread four green beads and three green sequins alternately on to the long wire. Glue the last bead to the sequin beside it. For each branch, alternate green beads and green sequins over approximately 3cm (1¼in) gluing the bead at the end of each branch to the sequin beside it. When the glue is dry trim the excess wire. Assemble the picture (see steps 7–8, page 12).

Sequinned patchwork ★★★

MATERIALS REQUIRED 🪙

TO MAKE ONE 30CM (12IN)
SQUARE CUSHION

- *9 × 12cm (4³/₄in) silk squares: 2 × lime green, 2 × gold green, 2 × dark orange, 2 × bright orange, 1 × dark red*
- *24cm (9¹/₂in) of 1cm (³/₈in) wide green satin ribbon*
- *24cm (9¹/₂in) of 2cm (³/₄in) wide sheer orange ribbon*
- *24cm (9¹/₂in) of 1cm (³/₈in) wide purple satin ribbon*
- *12cm (4³/₄in) of 2cm (³/₄in) wide sheer green ribbon*
- *embroidery thread in orange, turquoise, purple, yellow and light green*
- *3 washers (inner diameter 1.25cm (¹/₂in))*
- *1 washer (inner diameter 0.6cm (¹/₄in))*
- *1 sheet thick aluminium or flexible mirror*
- *1 fine needle*
- *small sequins in orange, pale green, turquoise and purple*
- *1 white dressmaker's pencil*
- *square sequins in silver*
- *orange and silver stars*
- *large sequins in vivid pink*
- *32cm (12³/₄in) square of deep red silk*
- *30cm (12in) square of thick wadding*

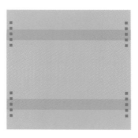

① Take one of the gold green silk squares and sew on two 12cm (4³/₄in) lengths of green satin ribbon, 2.5cm (1in) from the edges of the fabric. Take one of the bright orange squares and sew on two 12cm (4³/₄in) lengths of sheer orange ribbon 3.5cm (1³/₈in) from the edges of the fabric. Centre a length of purple ribbon on top of the orange ribbon and sew in place. Centre the sheer green ribbon on one of the lime green squares and sew in place.

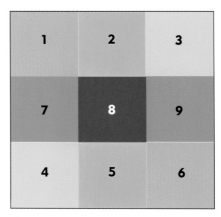

1	2	3
7	8	9
4	5	6

② Following the colour scheme in the diagram above, assemble the squares in three rows of three squares, allowing 1cm (³/₈in) for the seams. Sew the rows together following the diagram. Iron the seams open on the reverse.

Take care when ironing fabric embroidered with sequins: avoid touching the sequins, as they will melt on contact with a hot iron.

③ Cover each of the larger washers with a tight blanket stitch using orange, purple and turquoise embroidery thread (see diagram above). Secure the start and end threads by threading them through the stitches with a needle on the reverse of the washer. Cut 3 x 1.5cm (⁵/₈in) circles from the aluminium sheet for the three large mirrors and a 1.25cm (¹/₂in) circle for the small mirror. Cover the smaller washer with blanket stitch using green embroidery thread.

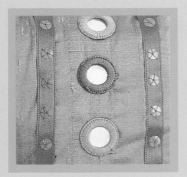

Square 1

Sew five orange sequins on the green satin ribbons using a strand of purple thread. Place the mirror circles beneath the large covered washers and secure with a strand of the same colour thread.

Square 2

Draw an eight-pointed star with 6.5cm (2½in) arms in the centre of the bright orange silk square. Sew on small purple sequins using two strands of orange thread.

Square 3

Sew six orange stars on the sheer green ribbon using two strands of yellow thread. Add green sequins either side of the ribbon using two strands of orange thread for some, turquoise for others.

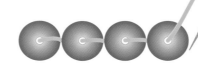

Square 4

Sew a scattering of sequins on the lime green silk square using two strands of orange embroidery thread, and some orange stars with two strands of turquoise thread, using the same stitch as in square 3.

Square 5

Stitch three silver stars between the two purple ribbons using two strands of turquoise thread. Sew four large vivid pink sequins on each of the ribbons using two strands of green thread.

Square 6

Sew six orange sequins randomly over the gold green silk square using two strands of orange thread. Circle each sequin with eight lazy daisy stitches (see page 8) using two strands of turquoise thread.

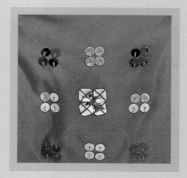

Square 7

Working outwards from the centre of the dark orange silk square, draw a spiral with the dressmaking pencil. Sew on your purple sequins using two strands of turquoise thread.

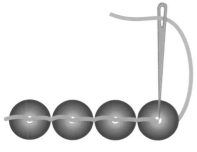

Square 8

Sew the small green washer and mirror in the centre of the dark red silk square. Draw a 6cm (2³/₈in) square around it with the dressmaker's pencil. Embroider with fly stitch (see page 9) using two strands of yellow thread and adding orange and purple sequins.

Square 9

Sew four silver square sequins in the centre of the dark orange silk square using two strands of orange thread. Following the pattern above sew on 4 x 4 turquoise sequins, 2 x 4 purple sequins and 2 x 4 pink sequins using two strands of turquoise or purple thread.

❹ Sew the square of deep red silk and patchwork right sides together allowing a 2cm (³/₄in) seam and leaving a 12cm (4³/₄in) opening. Iron the seams open. Place the wadding inside the cushion and close the opening with ladder stitch (see page 9).

❺ Create a quilted effect by sewing a vivid pink sequin in all four corners of the central square on both the front and back of the cushion. Attach the sequins with two strands of orange thread, using the stitch shown in square 1.

Beaded lampshade

MATERIALS REQUIRED

- *49.5 × 32cm (19^{1}/$_{2}$ × 12^{3}/$_{4}$in) yellow cotton voile*
- *orange and yellow thread*
- *sewing needle*
- *15cm (6in) round lampshade fitting*
- *dressmaker's pencil*
- *6 strips of orange cotton voile, 27 × 8cm (10^{3}/$_{4}$ × 3^{1}/$_{8}$in)*
- *fabric glue*
- *small glass beads and faceted beads in lime green, orange-pink and gold and six large beads in matching colours*
- *transparent mauve sequins*

1 Place the long edges of the yellow cotton voile right sides together and sew allowing a 2cm (³/₄in) seam. Iron the seam open. Turn the right side out and place the fabric cylinder over the round lampshade fitting. Fold the fabric over the top of the circle, allowing a 2cm (³/₄in seam) and make small slots to accommodate the crossbars. Pin the fabric in place.

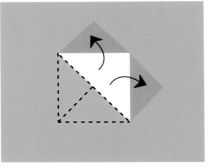

2 Using the dressmaker's pencil mark a 2.5cm (1in) square 7cm (2³/₄in) from the bottom of each of the orange voile strips. Cut two diagonal lines across the centre of each square and carefully turn and stick the triangles to the back of the fabric using fabric glue.

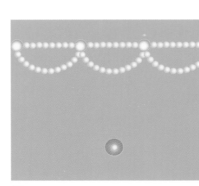

3 Outline the diamond shapes created with small glass beads adding a faceted bead in each corner. Alternate the bead colours on each voile strip. Sew a mauve sequin 2.5cm (1in) from the upper and lower points of the diamond, adding a bead of the same colour as that used for the diamond to the centre of each.

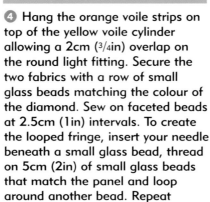

4 Hang the orange voile strips on top of the yellow voile cylinder allowing a 2cm (³/₄in) overlap on the round light fitting. Secure the two fabrics with a row of small glass beads matching the colour of the diamond. Sew on faceted beads at 2.5cm (1in) intervals. To create the looped fringe, insert your needle beneath a small glass bead, thread on 5cm (2in) of small glass beads that match the panel and loop around another bead. Repeat around the circle.

5 Hang a beaded pendant between each panel: thread on 12cm (4³/₄in) of faceted beads. Add a large matching bead then bring the thread back through the faceted beads and sew between each panel at the top of the lampshade.

Decorative photo frames **

MATERIALS REQUIRED

- *16cm (6¹/4in) square picture frame (picture size 8cm (3¹/8in) square)*
- *16cm (6¹/4in) square blue felt*
- *white dressmaker's pencil*
- *75cm (29¹/2in) of 1cm (³/8in) wide dark green satin ribbon*
- *75cm (29¹/2in) of 0.6cm (¹/4in) wide turquoise blue satin ribbon*
- *50cm (20in) of 1.5cm (⁵/8in) wide lime green ribbon*
- *50cm (20in) of 1cm (³/8in) wide green khaki ribbon*
- *fabric glue*
- *large flat sequins in metallic green*
- *green and blue faceted beads*
- *small flat sequins in pale iridescent green*
- *small clear blue-green glass beads*
- *small opaque blue-green glass beads*
- *large faceted sequins in metallic turquoise blue*
- *small transparent green faceted sequins*
- *green bugles*
- *turquoise blue thread*
- *1 fine needle*
- *Caribbean blue paint*

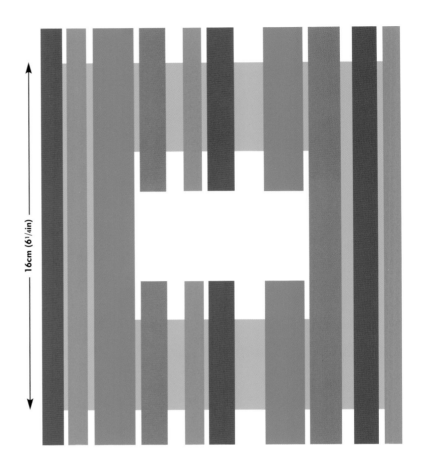

16cm (6¹/4in)

❶ Place the frame face down on the felt and trace around the picture aperture with the dressmaker's pencil. Cut out this square. Following the colour guide above, cut the ribbons into 22cm (8³/4in) lengths for decorating the sides and 11cm (4³/8in) lengths for the central sections. Pin them to the felt, leaving 3cm (1¹/4in) overhang top and bottom.

❷ Stick one end of each ribbon to the back of the felt with fabric glue. Turn the felt over and stick the ribbons down on the front of the felt.

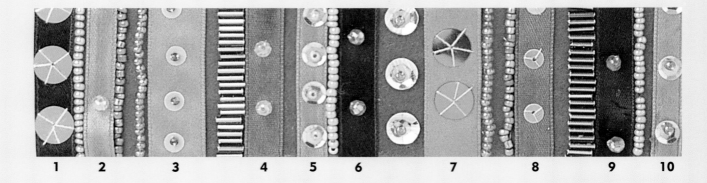

1   2   3   4   5   6   7   8   9   10

Ribbon 1
Sew on large green sequins at 1.5cm (5/8in) intervals with a five-pointed star, as shown above.

Ribbon 2
Sew on a green faceted bead at 3cm (1 1/4in) intervals.

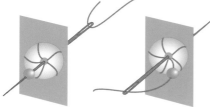

Ribbon 3
Sew on a small green sequin adding a green bead to the centre of each at 1cm (3/8in) intervals.

Ribbon 4
Sew on two green faceted beads at 1.5cm (5/8in) intervals.

Ribbon 5
Sew on a pale green sequin adding a small green glass bead to the centre of each at 1cm (3/8in) intervals.

Ribbon 6
Sew on two blue faceted beads at 1.5cm (5/8in) intervals.

Ribbon 7
Sew on two large sequins on the top and bottom sections of the frame using a five-pointed star.

Ribbon 8
Sew on small flat pale green sequins at 1.5cm (5/8in) intervals using a three-pointed star.

Ribbon 9
Sew on blue faceted beads at 2.5cm (1in) intervals.

Ribbon 10
Sew on green faceted sequins adding a small green glass bead to the centre of each, at 1.5cm (5/8in) intervals.

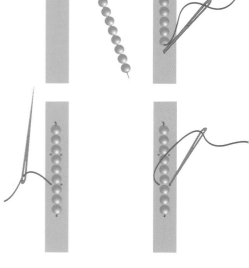

3 Decorate the spaces between ribbons 1 and 2, 2 and 3, 5 and 6, 7 and 8, and 9 and 10 with rows of small glass beads. Bring the needle through from the reverse of the felt at the top or bottom next to a ribbon. Thread on nine beads and bring the needle back to the reverse after the final bead. Bring the needle up to the left of the third bead and sew a stitch to the right, then come up to the left of the sixth bead and sew a stitch to the right: this will help to hold the beads securely. Continue in this way until the row is complete.

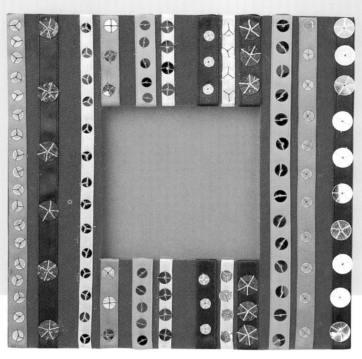

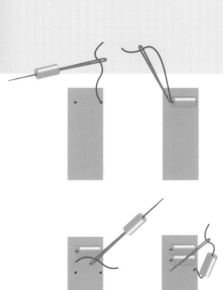

Vary the colour of the ribbons, sequins, beads and felt that you use to create a different look. In this example only the ribbons, and not the spaces between, have been decorated, leaving more of the felt to show through.

④ Decorate the spaces between ribbons 3 and 4, and 8 and 9 with rows of green bugles. Push the needle through from the reverse of the fabric at the appropriate point, thread on a bugle and take the needle back to the reverse of the fabric at the end of the bugle. Repeat this pattern as you work down the row. Decorate the space between ribbons 6 and 7 with large sequins.

⑤ Stick the remaining ends of the ribbons to the reverse of the felt. Paint the inside and outside edges of the picture frame and leave to dry. Apply glue to the surface of the frame and stick the decorated felt frame to it.

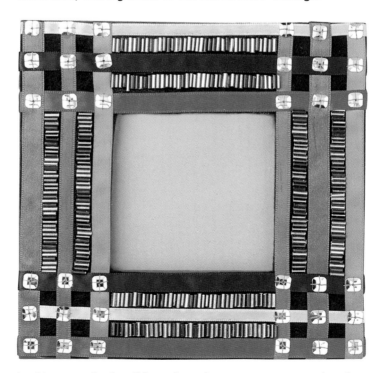

In this example the ribbons have been woven over and under each other before being glued to the felt. Square sequins highlight the weaving and bugles add a colourful touch.

Lace candle jars

MATERIALS REQUIRED

ORANGE LACE COVER
- *jar*
- *tape measure*
- *7cm (2³/4in) wide lace with scalloped edge*
- *coloured ink in red and yellow*
- *a small paint roller*
- *orange organdie*
- *small round beads in pink*
- *small clear glass beads in orange*
- *faceted beads in orange*
- *transparent sequins in orange*
- *thread to match the lace*
- *spray adhesive*
- *fabric glue*

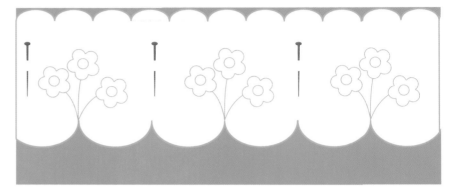

1 Measure the circumference of the jar and cut a length of lace to match plus 1.25cm (¹/2in). Lay the lace on a sheet of paper. Add ten drops of red ink and two drops of yellow ink to a dish, dilute with a little water and dab the paint roller in it. Paint both sides of the lace and hang up to dry.

2 Cut out two strips of orange organdie the same length as the circumference of the jar plus 1.25cm (¹/2in), and the same height. Pin the lace to one strip aligning the top edges, and outline the lace scallops by sewing on the small round pink beads. Next, decorate the middle section of the lace with glass and faceted beads. Sew on a transparent sequin decorated with a bead in the middle at regular intervals (see page 22). Sew small round beads and some faceted beads on to the bottom edge of the lace.

To place candles in tall jars, push a skewer into your candle, light the candle and place it at the bottom of the jar using the skewer. Use a second skewer to pull out the first skewer.

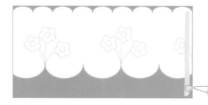

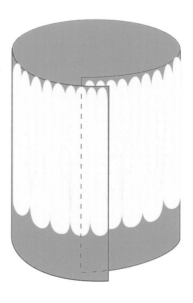

3 Spray adhesive on the second strip of organdie and stick the two pieces of fabric together. Apply a 0.6cm (¹/4in) strip of fabric glue down the length of the organdie and stick the ends together to make a cylinder. Slip the decorated fabric over the outside of the jar and place a tealight inside.

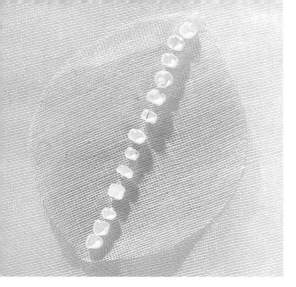

Beaded curtain*

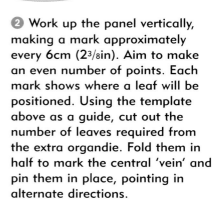

MATERIALS REQUIRED

- *organdie panel to fit your window plus 15cm (6in) for the leaves*
- *white dressmaker's pencil*
- *small glass beads in iridescent white*
- *white thread*
- *a needle*
- *large transparent sequins*

① Draw a vertical line 6cm (2³/₈in) from each side of the organdie panel using the dressmaker's pencil. Draw a third line in the middle of these two, giving the three lines on which to place the leaves.

② Work up the panel vertically, making a mark approximately every 6cm (2³/₈in). Aim to make an even number of points. Each mark shows where a leaf will be positioned. Using the template above as a guide, cut out the number of leaves required from the extra organdie. Fold them in half to mark the central 'vein' and pin them in place, pointing in alternate directions.

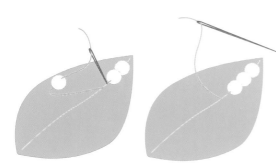

③ Sew on the leaves by embroidering a row of iridescent white beads along the central vein of each leaf. Check that the stitches are correctly aligned on the reverse of the fabric, as they will be seen from outside the window.

④ Sew around thirty sequins on to the curtain in a random pattern, securing the sequins with beads on both sides. Insert the needle from the reverse of the fabric to the front; leaving 4cm (1¹/₂in) of thread on the back of the fabric, thread on the sequin and the

bead, go back through the sequin, thread on another bead then tie a tight knot between the thread on the needle and the thread on the reverse of the fabric. Cut the threads at the base. Iron the curtain carefully on the reverse before hanging it.

Funky flower hat

MATERIALS REQUIRED

- *shisha mirrors in green, orange, pink, mauve and turquoise*
- *5 × 12cm (4³⁄₄in) lengths of 1cm (³⁄₈in) wide satin ribbon in purple, khaki, orange, pink and turquoise*
- *5 large sew-on jewels*
- *large round or faceted beads in pink, green, turquoise, orange and vivid pink*
- *small flat sequins in pink, turquoise, blue, purple and orange*
- *diamond-shaped studs in turquoise, green, pink, purple and clear*
- *5 flower-, leaf- and round-shaped buttons*
- *a few green bugles*
- *orange, turquoise, green, pink and fuchsia pink felt*
- *5 large sequins*
- *small opaque glass beads in green, pink, orange, turquoise and purple*
- *velvet or cotton hat*
- *needle and assorted threads*

> **How you decorate your hat will depend on the beads, buttons and other embellishments you have.** The above list of materials is offered as a guide, and your choice of colours will vary according to your taste.

1 Divide the circumference of the hat into five equal sections. Prepare five shisha mirrors (see pages 14 and 16). To make a rose, take one length of satin ribbon and fold it over at a right angle at one end, then wrap the ribbon twice around the fold and sew a couple of stitches at the base of the flower to secure. Keep wrapping the ribbon around, gradually loosening your grip as you wind and stitching again at the base to secure. To finish, fold the end of the ribbon in at a right angle and tie the thread in a knot. Repeat to make five roses.

2 Sew the embellishments on in the following order: one sew-on jewel surrounded by round beads; one shisha mirror set in a circle of small sequins secured with beads; one rose with two diamond-shaped studs; one button (or a design incorporating a button); one 1.5cm (⁵⁄₈in) felt disc secured with a large sequin and bead and encircled by opaque beads. Repeat this pattern as you work around your hat, varying the colours as you go.

Denim, fringes and beads**

MATERIALS REQUIRED

FRINGED DENIM BAG
- *denim fabric 48 × 29cm (19 × 11½in)*
- *1.56m (5ft 2in) of 1.5cm (⅝in) wide grosgrain ribbon in vivid pink*
- *1 blue dressmaker's pencil*
- *1 fine needle*
- *pink and dark blue thread*
- *small blue sequins with clear turquoise facets*
- *small glass beads in clear lime green*
- *large round beads in iridescent vivid pink*
- *small faceted sequins in dark blue*
- *small glass beads in dark blue*

To strengthen the bag handles, fold them in half 3cm (1¼in) from the bag edge and stitch along the length.

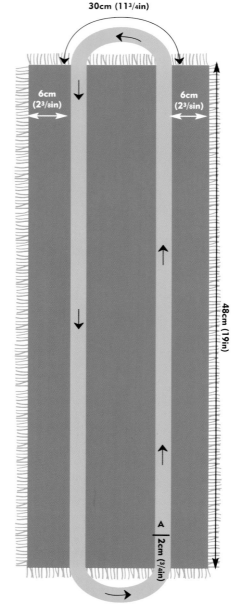

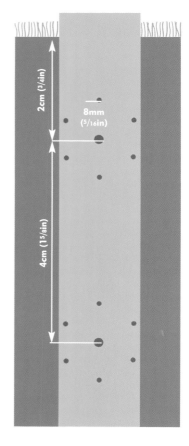

Sew a small popper into the inside of the bag behind a sequin **to enable you to close it.**

❶ Make a fringe 0.6cm (¼in) deep on all four sides of the denim. Position the grosgrain ribbon on the denim as shown above, and sew in place starting and finishing at A.

❷ Mark the grosgrain ribbon with the dressmaker's pencil 2cm (¾in) from the top fringe on both sides, and then at 4cm (1⅝in) intervals to make ten flower centres on each length of ribbon. Mark six petal points around each one as shown above.

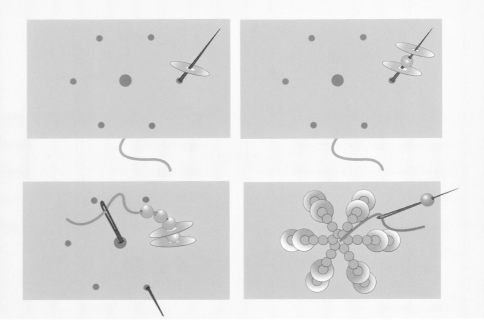

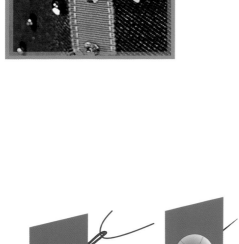

❸ Embroider the flowers using pink thread. Push the needle through from the wrong side of the fabric at one of the petal points. Thread on a turquoise blue sequin, hollow side towards the fabric, then a green glass bead and another sequin with the hollow side facing upwards.

Thread on three beads and insert your needle into the centre of the flower. Come up at the mark for the next petal. Repeat this pattern to create the six petals of the flower. Bring the needle out at the centre of the flower, thread on a large pink bead and go back through the flower centre to create the flower head.

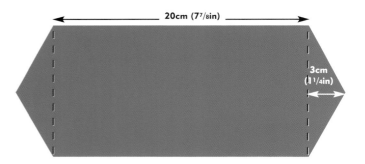

20cm (7⁷/₈in)

3cm (1¹/₄in)

❹ Use the blue thread to sew dark blue sequins randomly over the bag, keeping a distance of roughly 2cm (³/₄in) between each one. Secure each sequin hollow side up with a bead.

❺ Sew the bag up by stitching two side seams 0.6cm (¹/₄in) inside the fringes. Turn the bag upside down and fold a 3cm (1¹/₄in) triangle out of each side of the base of the bag. Stitch along the base to create the bottom of the bag as shown.

MATERIALS REQUIRED

MOBILE TELEPHONE HOLDER
- *denim fabric 30 × 10cm (12 × 4in), or to fit your mobile telephone*
- *30cm (11¾in) pink grosgrain ribbon*
- *same beads and sequins as for the denim bag*

1 Make a fringe 0.6cm (¼in) deep on all four sides of the denim fabric. Working lengthways, mark a line down the centre of the denim with the dressmaker's pencil. Centre the grosgrain ribbon over this line and stitch in place.

2 Mark the ribbon 7cm (2¾in) from the upper edge. From the centre of the ribbon draw a 2.5cm (1in) diameter circle. Divide the circle into six equal sections, then divide each section in half and mark a point midway along the length of each radius (see right).

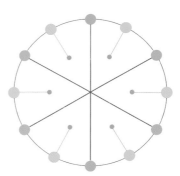

3 Embroider the flowers using pink thread. Push the needle through from the wrong side of the fabric at one of the petal points (marked in green on the diagram above right). Thread on a turquoise blue sequin, hollow side towards the fabric, then a green glass bead and another sequin with the hollow side facing upwards. Thread on three beads and insert your needle into the centre of the flower. Come up at the mark for the next petal. Repeat this pattern to create the six petals of the flower.

Bring the needle out at a pink point on the diagram above right. Embroider the motif again, using the same method and taking the needle back in at the midway point on the radius as shown on the diagram. Repeat for the six shorter petals then bring the needle out at the centre of the flower, thread on a large pink bead and go back through the centre of the flower to create the flower head.

4 Sew the blue sequins and beads randomly on to the telephone holder (see page 32, step 4). Fold the holder in half widthways, right sides together, and stitch the sides up allowing a 0.6cm (¼in) seam inside the fringes.

Organza scarves

MATERIALS REQUIRED

PLUM SCARF

- *36 × 130cm (14in × 4ft 3in) plum-coloured organza*
- *white dressmaker's pencil*
- *beads in bronze and deep red*
- *sequins in fuchsia, gold and purple*
- *1 fine needle*
- *plum-coloured thread*

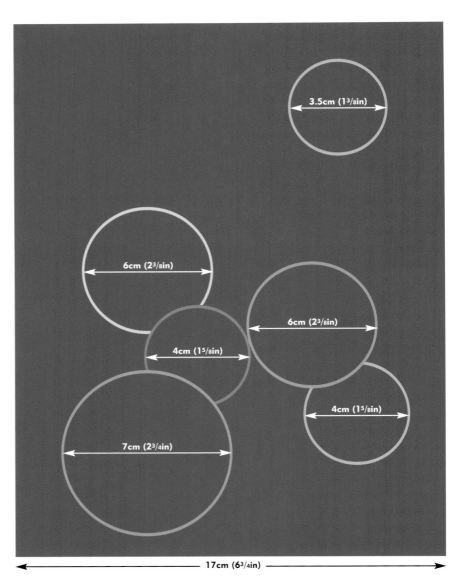

3.5cm (1³/₈in)

6cm (2³/₈in)

6cm (2³/₈in)

4cm (1⁵/₈in)

4cm (1⁵/₈in)

7cm (2³/₄in)

17cm (6³/₄in)

1 Fold the fabric in half lengthways and mark the halfway crease with the dressmaker's pencil.

2 Enlarge the template above by 112%, place it beneath your fabric aligning the edges at one side of the organza strip, and trace off the motifs with the dressmaker's pencil.

3 Sew the beads on individually (see diagram left) working in concentric circles until the two 4cm (1⁵/₈in) circles are full, and the top small circle has four layers of beads.

4 Sew on sequins in concentric circles following the template above. (Use technique shown on page 16, square 2.) Fold scarf in half, wrong sides together, and sew up using ladder stitch (see page 9).

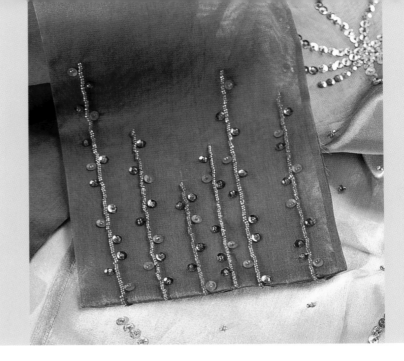

MATERIALS REQUIRED

MAROON SCARF

- *36 × 130cm (14in × 4ft 3in) organza in maroon*
- *white dressmaker's pencil*
- *small glass beads in purple, dark orange and deep red*
- *sequins in deep red, matte red and purple*
- *1 fine needle*
- *maroon thread*

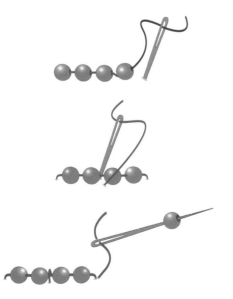

① Fold the fabric in half lengthways and mark the halfway crease. Following the diagram right, as a guide, mark the vertical lines on one half of the scarf with the white dressmaker's pencil.

② Bring the needle up from the wrong side of the fabric and thread on four beads. Take the needle back to the wrong side then come back up and sew a small loop between the second and third beads. Bring the needle back up in front of the final bead. (See diagram left.) Continue in this way until you have lines of beads matching the diagram above right.

③ Sew sequins randomly along the lines alternating the colours used. Secure each one with a bead (see page 22, ribbon 3).

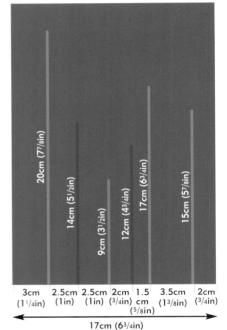

3cm (1¼in)	2.5cm (1in)	2.5cm (1in)	2cm (¾in)	1.5 cm (⅝in)	3.5cm (1⅜in)	2cm (¾in)

17cm (6¾in)

④ Fold the scarf in half lengthways, wrong sides together, and stitch up the sides using a 1.5mm (¹⁄₁₆in) seam. Do not sew up the two selvages. Turn the scarf right sides together. Sew a second seam 3mm (¹⁄₈in) from the edge, and sew up one of the ends. Turn the scarf wrong sides together and sew up the other end using ladder stitch (see page 9).

MATERIALS REQUIRED

KHAKI SCARF
- *sequins in maroon, orange and gold*
- *small glass beads in deep red, bronze and gold*
- *36 × 130cm (14in × 4ft 3in) organza in khaki*
- *1 fine needle*
- *khaki thread*
- *white dressmaker's pencil*

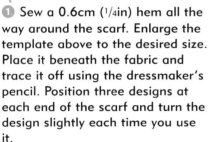

① Sew a 0.6cm (¹/₄in) hem all the way around the scarf. Enlarge the template above to the desired size. Place it beneath the fabric and trace it off using the dressmaker's pencil. Position three designs at each end of the scarf and turn the design slightly each time you use it.

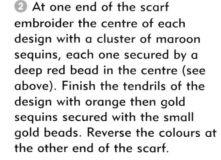

② At one end of the scarf embroider the centre of each design with a cluster of maroon sequins, each one secured by a deep red bead in the centre (see above). Finish the tendrils of the design with orange then gold sequins secured with the small gold beads. Reverse the colours at the other end of the scarf.

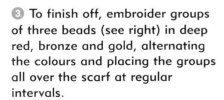

③ To finish off, embroider groups of three beads (see right) in deep red, bronze and gold, alternating the colours and placing the groups all over the scarf at regular intervals.

Printed fabric designs

NOTEBOOK JACKET
- *1 notebook of your choice*
- *tracing paper and pencil*
- *blue fabric printed with butterflies*
- *dressmaker's pencil*
- *sequins and beads in red, purple, mauve, dark blue and pink*
- *blue ribbon*
- *1 fine needle*
- *blue thread*
- *wadding and fabric glue*

1 Make a frame the size of the open notebook on tracing paper. Move the tracing paper frame around on the fabric to find an attractive design. The design does not necessarily have to be complete. Outline the frame on the fabric with dressmaker's pencil.

2 Select beads and sequins that match the colours of the fabric and use them to create a design on the fabric that complements and accentuates the printed design. Sew light coloured sequins on to dark areas and dark coloured sequins on to light areas. Fill some areas with patches of sequins and sew on others more sparingly, leaving some areas untouched so that the design does not look too busy. (For sewing on beads and sequins, see the techniques on pages 16 and 22.)

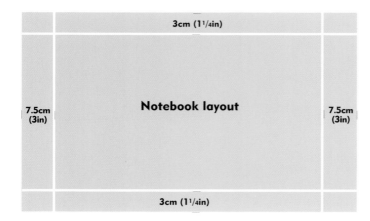

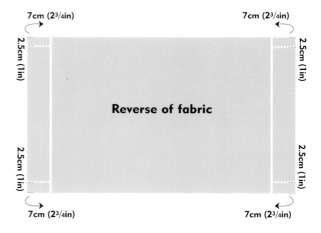

3 Add 7.5cm (3in) to the width of the marked rectangle and 3cm (1¼in) to the height, on both sides. Cut out. Sew a 0.6cm (¼in) hem around the outside edges to prevent fraying.

Stick two rectangles of wadding on to the front and back covers of the notebook using fabric glue.

4 Fold the two 7cm (2¾in) side flaps, right sides together, then fold the upper and lower edges under and sew a 2.5cm (1in) seam. Turn the fabric the right way out and iron. Sew a length of ribbon on the inside of each side flap, in the centre. Slide the notebook into its jacket.

MATERIALS REQUIRED

VANITY PURSE
- *sequins and beads in purple, turquoise and pink*
- *white sequins*
- *clear beads in gold and orange*
- *flower printed fabric*
- *pink ribbon*
- *1 fine needle*
- *pink thread*

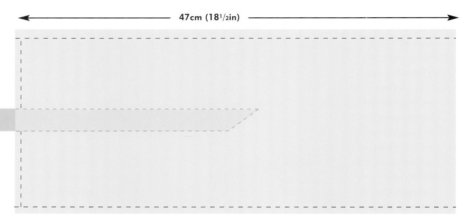

47cm (18¹/₂in)

① Locate a design in the same way as for the notebook jacket (see page 38, step 1). Cut out two rectangles of fabric 22 x 47cm (8³/₄ x 18¹/₂in). Embroider a design on one of the fabric strips using the beads and sequins to outline the fabric design (see page 38, step 2).

② Place the two rectangles right sides together and stitch around three edges, as shown above, using a 1cm (³/₈in) seam. Incorporate a length of pink ribbon into the stitching on the short edge. Turn the fabric right side out. Insert a rectangle of wadding 20 x 45cm (8 x 18in). Fold in the edges on the unstitched side and sew together close to the edge.

③ Divide the folder into three. Fold the bottom third of the holder up and sew the outside edges together using blanket stitch (see page 8). Centre and sew a second length of ribbon for a fastening.

MATERIALS REQUIRED

1 Choose and embroider a design on the printed fabric rectangle (see page 38, step one). Arrange the sequins in groups according to their colour. Use the beads to create lines.

2 Place the embroidered and plain fabric rectangles right sides together and sew up using 0.6cm (¹/₄in) seams. Leave one of the sides open. Turn the fabric the right way out and iron carefully to flatten out the seams.

3 Insert the rectangle of wadding then fold in the open edges 0.6cm (¹/₄in) and sew 3mm (¹/₈in) from the edge.

4 Fold the bag in half, plain fabric on the inside, and sew up the two outside edges with visible stitching 3mm (¹/₈in) from the edge. Fold the cord in half and sew the two halves together using pink beads at approximately 2cm (³/₄in) intervals. Sew the strap to the inside of the bag.

SHOULDER BAG

- *20 × 48cm (7⁷/₈ × 19in) rectangle printed fabric*
- *sequins in blue, white and green*
- *small glass beads in blue, white, green and pink*
- *faceted beads in pink*
- *pink bugles*
- *20 × 48cm (7⁷/₈ × 19in) rectangle pink fabric*
- *18 × 46cm (7 × 18in) rectangle wadding*
- *220cm (7ft 2¹/₂in) thin cord in pink*

Flowery belts ★★

MATERIALS REQUIRED

RED SILK BELT

- *24 × 84cm (9¹/₂ × 33in) red wild silk*
- *4 × 25cm (10in) lengths of red cord*
- *thread and needle*
- *6 × 60cm (2³/₈ × 24in) red velvet*
- *iron-on fabric in black or red*
- *washers (interior diameter 0.6cm (¹/₄in))*
- *1 sheet thick aluminium or flexible mirror*
- *red embroidery thread*
- *small glass beads in iridescent red and maroon*
- *bugles in iridescent red*
- *8 large flat sequins in red*
- *faceted maroon beads*

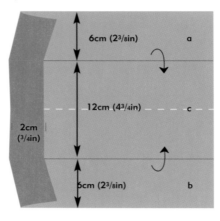

① Fold the silk as indicated in the diagram left: fold in 2cm (³/₄in) along each shorter edge, then fold a and b up to line c. Fold in half again at line c to create a 6cm (2³/₈in) strip. Position two lengths of cord inside each end of the silk strip, 2cm (³/₄in) apart, and sew around all the edges of the silk 3mm (¹/₈in) from the edge, trapping the cord inside.

② Trace around the small flower template (see page 64), then cut out nine red flowers backed with iron-on fabric (see page 45, step 1). Prepare nine mirrors (see page 14). Sew a small mirror in the centre of each flower and decorate the flowers with sequins, beads and bugles using the diagrams left as a guide.

③ Sew the flowers on to the belt at evenly spaced intervals using a faceted maroon bead between each petal. Sew a large red sequin secured with a bead (see page 22) between each flower.

MATERIALS REQUIRED

BLACK FLOWER

- *15 × 30cm (6 × 12in) black fleece*
- *tracing paper and thin card*
- *dressmaker's pencil*
- *small bugles in iridescent black*
- *large faceted beads in iridescent black*
- *small glass beads in black*
- *faceted sequins in blue marine*
- *small faceted beads in iridescent black*
- *large bugles in iridescent black*
- *1.5m (5ft) of 2cm (³⁄₄in) wide black velvet ribbon*
- *black thread*
- *a fine needle*

❶ Trace around the three flower templates (see page 64) and transfer them to the thin card. Lay the pieces of card on the fabric and draw around them. Cut them out carefully.

❷ Decorate the largest of the flowers with small iridescent black bugles and large faceted beads. The large faceted beads will be hidden by the flower above and will lift it slightly. Sew the small glass beads between the petals.

❸ For the medium-sized flower, sew on sequins secured by beads (see page 22), small faceted beads between the petals and large faceted beads at the centre.

❹ For the small flower, use iridescent black bugles and sew on small faceted beads between the petals.

❺ Stack the three flowers on top of one another. Insert your needle through the centre from the back of the fabric, thread on a large faceted bead which will act as the head of the flower, then go back through the same spot and finish off on the reverse of the fabric.

❻ Sew on the flower 35cm (14in) from one end of the ribbon: secure with a small stitch at the back of the flower head. Tie the ribbon belt with a knot just beneath the flower.

MATERIALS REQUIRED

RED FLOWER
- *15 × 30cm (6 × 12in) red velvet*
- *iron-on fabric in black*
- *tracing paper and thin card*
- *dressmaker's pencil*
- *small faceted sequins in vivid red*
- *small glass beads in iridescent red and maroon*
- *small faceted beads in maroon*
- *bugles in iridescent red*
- *1 large bead in iridescent red*
- *1.5m (5ft) of 1.5cm (⅝in) wide velvet ribbon in raspberry red*
- *red thread and a fine needle*

① Stick the iron-on fabric on the back of the velvet, following the manufacturer's instructions. Trace off the three flower templates (see page 64), transfer to thin card and cut. Lay the flowers on the velvet, draw around them and cut out.

② Decorate the largest flower with red sequins and beads and sew on a small faceted bead in maroon between each petal.

③ Decorate the middle flower with small glass beads in iridescent red and sew on a small faceted bead in maroon between each petal.

④ For the smallest of the flowers, sew on iridescent red bugles and a small faceted maroon bead in between each of the petals.

⑤ Layer the flowers and sew together at the centre with beaded tassels: using 6cm (2⅜in), 7cm (2¾in) and 3cm (1¼in) lengths of thread make up three beaded tassels with maroon beads (see page 18) and two with iridescent red beads 4cm (1⅝in) and 8cm (3⅛in) in length. Use a sequin in front of the last bead. Sew the flower on to the ribbon.

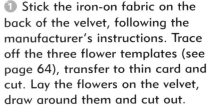

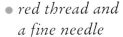

Slinky camisoles

MATERIALS REQUIRED

MAUVE CAMISOLE
- *small sequins in vivid pink and silver*
- *small opaque glass beads in mauve and purple*
- *small clear glass beads in pink and silver*
- *mauve thread*
- *a fine needle*

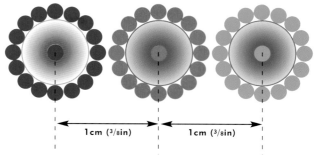

1cm (³/₈in)   1cm (³/₈in)

1 Follow the colour guide shown above and position each sequin flower as shown. Start from the bottom back of one of the straps, work across the front then up the second strap finishing at the back.

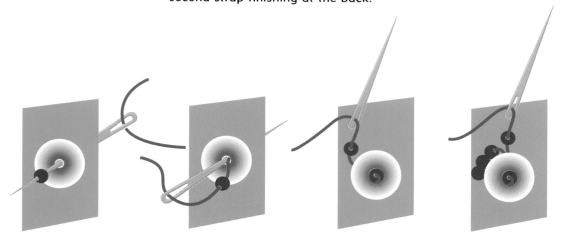

2 Thread the fine needle with 50cm (20in) mauve thread. Insert the needle from the back of the fabric, thread the sequin and then the bead onto the needle and push the needle back through the hole in the sequin. Secure with a small stitch on the back of the fabric, behind the sequin.

3 To create the petals, bring the needle out beside the sequin, thread on a purple bead, go back into the fabric immediately in front of the bead, then come up at the same spot to thread on the next bead. Repeat this pattern as you work around the sequin, then finish off by tying a small knot on the reverse of the fabric.

MATERIALS REQUIRED

SKY-BLUE CAMISOLE

- *small star-shaped sequins in silver*
- *small opaque glass beads in blue*
- *large clear beads in silver*
- *flat sequins in silver*
- *sky-blue thread*
- *a fine needle*

When you are moving between stars, especially when working on the straps, ensure that you do not pull the thread too tight, as this can cause the fabric to lose its elasticity.

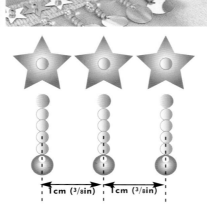

❶ Position the design as shown above. Start at the bottom back of a camisole strap, then work across the front and up the other strap finishing at the bottom back. First sew on stars then pendants.

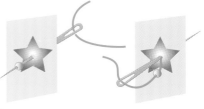

❷ Thread 50cm (20in) sky-blue thread on to a fine needle and push the needle through from the back of the fabric. Thread a star-shaped sequin and a blue bead onto your needle, then go back through the hole in the star. Secure the star with a small knot on the back of the fabric, behind the sequin. Sew the stars over the straps and front of the camisole.

❸ Using the dressmaker's pencil mark off 1cm (³/₈in) intervals just under the stars on the front of the vest. Bring the needle through from the back of the fabric at one of the marks and thread on a large silver bead, 4 small blue glass beads and a sequin – in that

order. Go through the sequin and back through the beads again. Take the needle to the back of the fabric at the mark, then bring it through to the right side at the next mark. Repeat this pattern all the way along the front neckline of the camisole.

MATERIALS REQUIRED

DEEP PINK CAMISOLE
- *small sequins in silver*
- *small opaque glass beads in pink*
- *small clear glass beads in pink and mauve*
- *large sequins in vivid pink*
- *deep pink thread and fine needle*

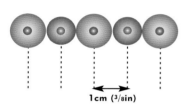

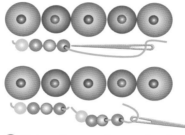

1 Position the design as shown above. Start at the bottom back of one of the camisole straps, then work across the front and up the other strap finishing at the bottom back. Alternate pink and silver sequins and attach each with an opaque pink bead (see page 48).

2 Below the sequins on the front neckline, sew a row of clear beads in alternating colours. Bring the needle through from the back of the fabric, thread on four beads and go back through the fabric immediately after the last bead. Bring the needle out at the same point, thread on four more beads. Repeat to end of neckline. Decorate the front of the top with a scattering of large pink sequins secured with beads.

BRACELET
- *60cm (24in) of 1.5cm (⅝in) wide mauve ribbon*
- *small round sequins and star-shaped sequins in silver*
- *small opaque glass beads in blue and purple*

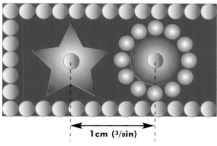

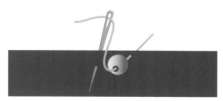

1 Measure your wrist and transfer the measurement to the centre of the ribbon. Sew on the main design, following the suggested layout above. (For techniques see pages 46 and 48.)

2 To create the border, sew beads on individually, sewing over the edge of the ribbon (see above). Secure the bracelet by knotting it around your wrist.

Evening T-shirts**

MATERIALS REQUIRED

FLYING BUTTERFLIES T-SHIRT
- *grey T-shirt*
- *white dressmaker's pencil*
- *tracing paper and thin card*
- *small glass beads in iridescent blue and green*
- *round beads in pearlized white*
- *6 sew-on jewels*
- *grey thread and fine needle*

1 Trace off the butterfly outline above, transfer to thin card and cut out.

Ensure that you do not pull too hard on the thread whilst embroidering the butterflies: this will prevent the fabric from gathering.

2 Lay the butterfly on your T-shirt and draw around the motif several times using the dressmaker's pencil and following the guide left. Add some antennae to your butterflies. Use the pencil to mark the positions of your sew-on jewels.

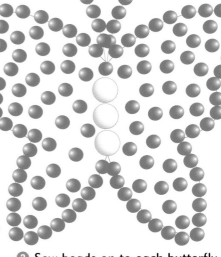

3 Sew beads on to each butterfly, starting with the outline and the white beads in the centre and tips of each antennae. Then fill in. Alternate between green and blue butterflies. Lastly, sew on the fake jewels.

MATERIALS REQUIRED

SINGLE BUTTERFLY MOTIF

- *plum T-shirt*
- *tracing paper and thin card*
- *white dressmaker's pencil*
- *small glass beads in clear pink*
- *faceted sequins in matte dark pink and purple*
- *small round beads in vivid pink*
- *plum-coloured thread*
- *a fine needle*

❶ Trace off the half butterfly template (see page 63) and transfer to thin card. Reverse the tracing to complete the butterfly. Cut out to make a template.

❷ Position the template on the centre front of the T-shirt 6cm (2³/₈in) below the neckline and draw around it with dressmaker's pencil.

❸ Outline the butterfly and antennae with small glass beads then fill in the butterfly with sequins, securing each one with a bead (see page 46). Use the diagram right as a colour guide. The butterfly's body is made using a row of vivid pink round beads and the ends of the antennae are pink sequins held in place with a round bead in vivid pink.

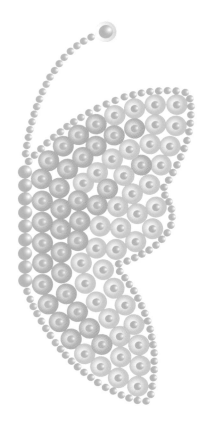

MATERIALS REQUIRED

BUTTERFLY BROOCH
- *black silk*
- *iron-on fabric in black*
- *dressmaker's pencil*
- *small glass beads in green*
- *1 sew-on jewel*
- *stick-on brooch clasp*
- *black thread*
- *a fine needle*

1 Stick the iron-on fabric on to the reverse of the silk following the manufacturer's instructions: this will lend stiffness to the fabric and help prevent fraying.

2 Trace around the butterfly outline on page 50, transfer to thin card and cut out. Place the butterfly on the black silk, draw around it and cut out carefully. Outline and fill in the butterfly with small glass beads (see page 50). Sew a fake jewel in the centre and stick a brooch clasp on the back.

Variations

SINGLE STAR T-SHIRT
Follow the instructions for the Single Butterfly Motif (see page 52), using orange beads, purple and orange sequins, pink thread and a fine needle.

SILVER AND BLACK
Follow the instructions for the Flying Butterfly T-shirt (see page 50), using small glass beads in silver, black thread and a fine needle and a sew-on jewel in the centre of each star: the stars can be arranged on the diagonal like the butterflies or in a straight line.

Embroidered pumps ★★

MATERIALS REQUIRED

- *small glass beads in mauve, purple, turquoise, lime green and pink*
- *bugles in dark pink, pale mauve, turquoise, lime green and purple*
- *square sequins*
- *sequins in dark pink, pale pink, purple, turquoise and green*
- *1 pair canvas pumps*
- *thread to match pumps*

1 For best results, work along the existing seams of the shoe. The varied elements that make up the design may be sewed on as follows: sew sequins on using a thread cross design (see page 22); thread beads on in rows of three or one at a time; hold square sequins in place with a bead; align bugles either horizontally or vertically in rows of three.

2 Sew different coloured beads in alternating colours (turquoise, pink, green, purple and mauve) around the upper edge of each shoe, using the seam as a guide.

3 Vary the ways in which you combine the sequins, beads and bugles, using the examples below for inspiration.

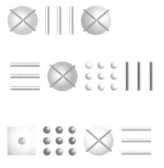

You can embroider the same type of design on other canvas shoes such as espadrilles or mules.

Glamorous trousers ★★★

MATERIALS REQUIRED

DECORATIVE BANDS

- *1.5cm (⁵/₈in) wide grosgrain ribbon in orange and maroon*
- *0.6cm (¹/₄in) wide satin ribbon in pink*
- *faceted beads in purple*
- *large sequins with side holes in purple*
- *embroidery thread in pink, orange and deep red*
- *small glass beads in orange and deep red*
- *bugles in orange and dark pink*
- *small faceted beads in deep red*
- *small faceted sequins in orange*
- *star-shaped, diamond-shaped, heart-shaped and square studs in purple*
- *large flat sequins in vivid pink*
- *matching threads*
- *a fine needle*
- *dressmaker's pencil*

You should always use strong thread for sewing on beads and sequins. Remember to turn garments inside out when washing.

1 Sew a length of orange grosgrain around the bottom of each leg, maroon grosgrain 4cm (1⁵/₈in) above the first and orange grosgrain 1cm (³/₈in) above that.

3 Decorate the lower edge of the maroon ribbon with a fringe. Space the pendants at 1cm (³/₈in) intervals and thread on an orange bead, one red, one orange, an orange or dark pink bugle, two orange beads, a red faceted bead and an orange bead. Take the needle and thread back through the beads and to the back of the fabric. Repeat.

5 On the top orange ribbon alternate between studs and large pink sequins, following the diagram above.

2 Decorate the first orange ribbon as follows: pin the pink satin ribbon 3mm (¹/₈in) from the upper edge. Sew it on using alternate purple beads and large purple sequins at approximately 1cm (³/₈in) intervals – see picture right. Embroider rows of chain stitch in deep red, pink and orange (see page 8) above the ribbon.

4 Using two strands of deep red embroidery thread, sew orange sequins on to the maroon ribbon at 2cm (³/₄in) intervals.

6 2cm (³/₄in) from the top of the second orange ribbon, draw a line with the dressmaker's pencil and embroider a chain stitch over the top in pink. Just below, sew on large purple sequins at 2cm (³/₄in) intervals.

MATERIALS REQUIRED

SHOOTING STARS

- *6 star-shaped sequins*
- *small silver and iridescent glass beads*
- *small white bugles*
- *white dressmaker's pencil*
- *tracing paper*
- *pencil*
- *a fine needle*
- *white thread*

HEART

- *small glass beads in turquoise and lime green*
- *flat sequins in turquoise*
- *small bugles in lime green*
- *heart-shaped stud in lime green*
- *turquoise thread*
- *a fine needle*
- *blue dressmaker's pencil*

① Trace off the shooting stars template (see page 64), go over it on the back with dressmaker's pencil. Place wrong side down on the fabric and pencil over the lines again, the motif will appear in white on the fabric. Touch it up to make it clear if needed.

② Sew the sequin stars on, securing with iridescent beads. Embroider the comet's tail as follows: on the first and fifth rows, sew iridescent beads on close together over roughly 8cm (3¹/₈in), then begin to space them out; on the second and fourth rows, sew white bugles on close together over roughly 8cm (3¹/₈in), then space them out; on the third row, sew silver beads on close together over roughly 8cm (3¹/₈in), and then space them out. To finish off, scatter eight iridescent beads at random between the star-shaped sequins.

① Trace off and transfer the heart template (see page 64 and step one above). Outline the heart with turquoise glass beads.

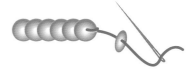

② Sew a row of overlapping turquoise sequins inside the row of beads.

③ Embroider a row of small green bugles, then a row of small green beads, then a row of small turquoise beads. Sew the heart-shaped stud in the centre of the heart and fill in around it with turquoise glass beads.

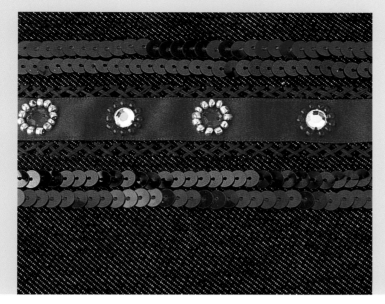

MATERIALS REQUIRED

SEQUINNED TROUSERS
- *1.5cm (⁵/₈in) wide satin ribbon in deep red*
- *embroidery thread in dark plum*
- *a needle*
- *red studs*
- *round sew-on jewels*
- *large glass beads in deep red and silver*
- *stitched sequins in red and plum*
- *red and purple thread*
- *dressmaker's pencil*

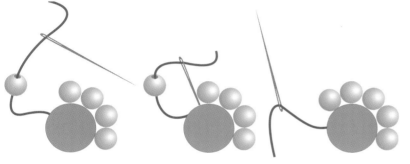

1 Sew on the deep red ribbon 4cm (1⁵/₈in) from the bottom of each trouser leg. Using the dressmaker's pencil, draw two lines 0.6cm (¹/₄in) from the bottom and top edge of the ribbon. Using the embroidery thread, embroider two rows of herringbone stitch (see page 9) 0.6cm (¹/₄in) in width.

2 At 3cm (1¹/₄in) intervals, sew alternating studs and fake jewels on to the ribbon. Sew red or silver beads around each one following the diagram above.

3 0.6cm (¹/₄in) from the rows of herringbone stitch, sew on two rows of stitched sequins: bring the needle from the back of the fabric through a sequin; stitch over the thread linking the sequins and come up through the next sequin. To speed up the process you could sew one sequin in every three.

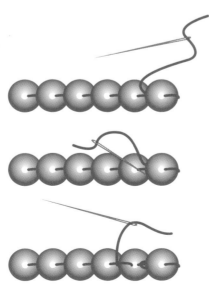

Sparkly sarongs ★★

MATERIALS REQUIRED

BLUE SARONG

- *blue cotton fabric 1m × 2m (3ft 3in × 6ft 6in)*
- *small clear glass beads in silver*
- *flat sequins in clear blue*
- *large round beads in iridescent white*
- *large sequins with side holes in silver*
- *1 fine needle*
- *blue thread*
- *1 dressmaker's pencil*
- *tracing paper and thin card*

1 Turn under and sew a small hem all around the fabric. Draw a band 6.5cm (2¹/₂in) wide 1.5cm (⁵/₈in) from the bottom edge using the dressmaker's pencil. Trace off the flower template (see page 63), transfer to thin card and cut out.

3 Outline the band and flowers with small silver beads, then fill in the spaces between the flowers. Bring the needle through from the back of the fabric and thread on a bead. Take the needle back to the reverse of the fabric then up again 3mm (¹/₈in) away (see right). Repeat until the spaces between the flowers are filled. Sew a blue sequin in the centre of each flower secured by a bead (see page 46).

2 Place the template on the fabric and trace around the motif, using the diagram above as a guide. Start from the right and draw out the flower as many times as is necessary to decorate the fabric.

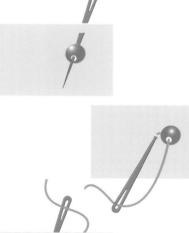

4 Using the dressmaker's pencil mark every 2cm (³/₄in) along the edge of the fabric under the bead flowers. Sew a sequin with a side hole at each mark (see left).

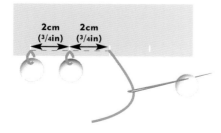

2cm (³/₄in) 2cm (³/₄in)

MATERIALS REQUIRED

ORANGE SARONG

- *small bronze beads*
- *small sequins in gold*
- *orange thread*
- *orange fabric*
- *1 fine needle*

❶ Use the bird template (see page 63) placed inside a 5cm (2in) wide band. (See page 60, steps 1–3.)

5cm (2in)

❷ To sew on the beaded fringe: mark the edge of the fabric at 1cm (³/₈in) intervals under the beaded birds. Bring the needle through from the back of the fabric hem, thread on three small beads, a sequin and another small bead. Go back through the sequin and beads. Push the needle into the hem and come up again at the next mark.

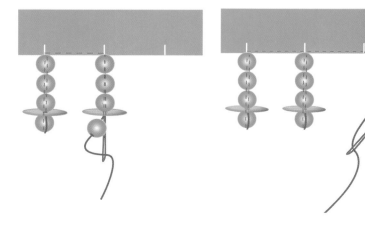

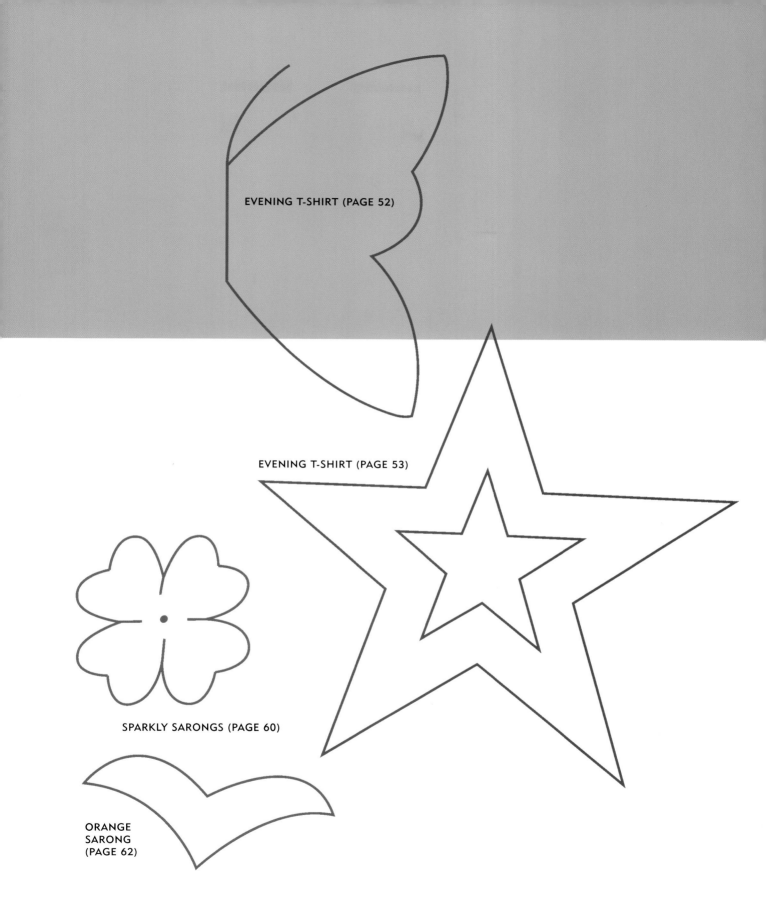

EVENING T-SHIRT (PAGE 52)

EVENING T-SHIRT (PAGE 53)

SPARKLY SARONGS (PAGE 60)

ORANGE
SARONG
(PAGE 62)

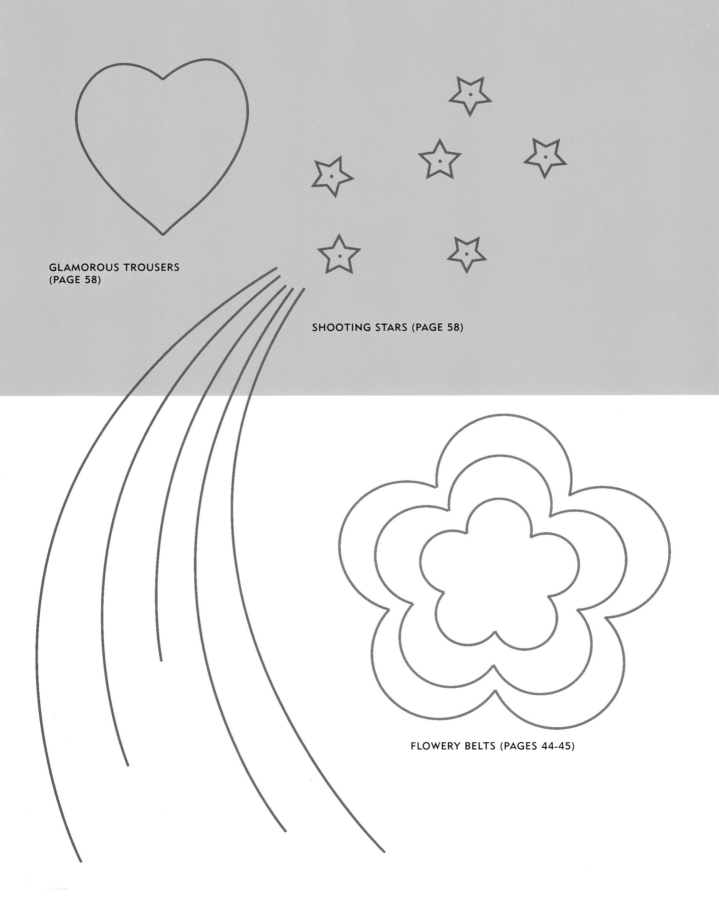

GLAMOROUS TROUSERS
(PAGE 58)

SHOOTING STARS (PAGE 58)

FLOWERY BELTS (PAGES 44-45)